ROBOTS IMPROVING INDUSTRY

WILL ROBOTS TAKE OVER THE WORLD?

Louise Spilsbury

CHERITON
CHILDREN'S BOOKS

Published in 2024 by **Cheriton Children's Books**
1 Bank Drive West, Shrewsbury, Shropshire, SY3 9DJ, UK

© 2024 Cheriton Children's Books

First Edition

Author: Louise Spilsbury
Designer: Paul Myerscough
Editor: Jennifer Sanderson
Proofreader: Katie Dicker

Picture credits: Cover: Shutterstock/Fotogenicstudio (top), Shutterstock/Asharkyu (bottom). Inside: p1: International Climbing Machines, p4: Shutterstock/Blue Planet Studio, p5: Shutterstock/Ociacia, p6: Flickr/The Lamb Family, p7: Shutterstock/Cineberg, p8l: Shutterstock/Dabarti CGI, p8r: Shutterstock/MikeDotta, p9: Shutterstock/Helloabc, p10: Shutterstock/MikeDotta, p11: Shutterstock/Photodiem, p12: Flickr/Failing Angel, p13: Shutterstock/Asharkyu, p14: Shutterstock/wi6995, p15: Wikimedia Commons/RoboGuru, p16b: Wikimedia Commons/Daimler und Benz Stiftung, p16c: Shutterstock/Gorodenkoff, p17: Shutterstock/Gorodenkoff, p18: ABB, p19: ABB, p20: Shutterstock/Dmitry Kalinovsky, p21: ZenRobotics, p22: Shutterstock/Sabisaftoiu, p23: Shutterstock/Bluesilent, p24: Wikimedia Commons/Oregon State University, p25b: Shutterstock/Petrmalinak, p25t: Shutterstock/MPH Photos, pp26-27: Yara Birkeland/CFC, p28: Lely Ireland, p29: Shutterstock/BB Design Stock, p30: Shutterstock/Scharfsinn, p31: Agrobot, p32: Carbon Robotics, p33: iBex Automation, p34: Shutterstock/Andy Dean Photography, p35: ProKASRO Mechatronik GmbH, p36b: Shutterstock/Jimi Knightley, p36c: International Climbing Machines, p37: Shutterstock/A Lesik, p38: Shutterstock/One Shutter One Memory, p39: Wikimedia Commons/Josselin Bequet, pp40-41: Shutterstock/Sergio Del Carpio Alamo, p40: Shutterstock/Scharfsinn, p41: Epiroc, p42l: Shutterstock/Timofeev Vladimir, p42r: Shutterstock/Lassedesignen, p43: Shutterstock/kckate16, p44: Wikimedia Commons/Richard Greenhill/Hugo Elias, p45: Shutterstock/Adam Vilimek.

Printed in China

Please visit our website,
www.cheritonchildrensbooks.com
to see more of our high-quality books.

CONTENTS

Chapter 1

ROBOTS AT WORK

One day in the future, there could be robots everywhere! As you walk around your neighborhood, you might see robots cleaning windows, greeting you in stores, and making food in a nearby diner. There will be robots delivering packages and robots in every grocery store. In fact, robots already work in many of the world's major industries and new robots are being invented every year to take on many of the jobs that people currently do.

ROBOTS OR PEOPLE

There are several reasons why companies want to buy and use more robots. After they have been **programmed** to do a particular job, robots will keep doing the same job in the same way until they are switched off. That means they never get bored or distracted, and they can produce more accurate and consistent work than humans. It also means that they rarely make mistakes as opposed to human workers. Robotic workers can work at the same speed and they have no need for lunch or breaks, days off, or vacations.

Humanoid robots are robots that look like people. Soon, these robots may be living and working alongside us.

SAFETY FIRST

Robots also help reduce the risk of people getting injured at work. For example, moving heavy goods and products using a **forklift** is dangerous work. Human operators can make mistakes when they are tired, sick, or get distracted by something. Robotic forklifts don't get tired. They are carefully controlled by highly advanced systems that map out the routes they take and the jobs that they do. Robotic forklifts have **sensors** to stop them colliding with obstacles or bumping into people. That means there is less chance of accidents that result in injuries.

One day, robots may be in charge of humans at work!

BIG BOT DEBATE

Are Robots Better or Worse for Workers?

Some people say that robots create better jobs for workers because robots cannot service or program themselves. Robots do the boring, repetitive jobs such as making goods on a factory floor, while people can work in more interesting roles such as programming the robots. Other people disagree. They believe robotic workers are taking away jobs from humans who need the work and wages. They say companies choose robots over people because they are cheaper but not necessarily better. Do you think robots improve jobs or do you think they harm them?

ROBOTS LEND A HAND

The simplest robots in industry are programmed to repeat basic tasks using moving parts, such as an arm. Robots like this can be found working behind the counter in diners and fast-food restaurants all over the world. They can chop ingredients, flip burgers, build pizzas, and perform many other tasks quickly and efficiently. These robots also greatly reduce the risk of human chefs burning or cutting themselves in a busy kitchen.

Robotic chefs can move burger patties into position on a griddle and keep track of each burger's cook-time and temperature.

ARMED FOR ACTION

In many ways, robotic arms are designed to work like a human arm. As in a human arm, the parts, or links, of the arm are connected by joints. These allow different parts of the arm to turn or move up and down, or left and right. At the tip of a robotic arm is an end effector. An end effector is a little like a human hand. The difference is that the robot's end effector can be fitted with different parts, from fingers and grippers to drills.

ROBO-CHEFS ON DUTY?

Customers ordering a burger and fries at some fast-food restaurants might be surprised to learn who's cooking their lunch! A large robotic arm takes frozen fries and other foods out of a freezer, dips them into hot oil, then puts the ready-to-serve product onto a tray. The arm can also cook and flip burgers and place them on trays when they are good to go. Robotic arms can even be programmed to clean griddle surfaces and equipment. In fact, these robotic arms can fry nearly any type of food on their own. Human workers place the food in a hopper and the robot uses **artificial intelligence (AI)** to automatically recognize and transfer the food. Then it fries the food to perfection.

Drink up! Robotic arms can serve drinks to many customers in a short period. Robots can brew coffee, make milk froth, and even pour syrups into paper cups.

truly
obot

ROBOTS RISING UP!

At some drive-thru fast-food outlets, ordering is done through kiosks or an app, not a human server with a friendly greeting or "Have a nice day!" And instead of human workers handing you a bag with a smile at the drive-thru, an automatic **conveyor belt** brings your order to a window. Some people say they miss seeing people when they have to use AI-powered voice systems like this and worry about the loss of jobs for humans.

ROBOT-RUN STORES

One day, we might be greeted by a friendly new robotic assistant when we enter a store. These robots are fitted with a camera to detect, or pick up, shoppers' faces. They also have speakers that they use to greet people in the customer's own language. The robots could find their way around complicated store floor plans and help customers find what they are looking for. Many may have an information display screen to show shoppers recommendations and additional information.

SHELF STACKERS

On busy weekends, it can be hard to keep a grocery store's shelves fully stocked. No sooner have they been filled, than customers have emptied them again. Robots such as Tally are designed to solve this problem. These fully **autonomous** robots roam store aisles alongside human shoppers during regular business hours. The robots check to see if there are enough goods on the shelves, and if they start to run out, they restock with new ones.

Robots work inside and outside stores, from greeting customers to keeping the stores clean, like this window-cleaning robot.

Robotic store assistants have a screen that gives customers all the information they need.

Robotic cleaners can mop large areas of floor efficiently and quickly and can work all hours, day and night, without needing to rest.

CONTROLLING ROBOTS

In some grocery stores, it might seem that a robot is autonomously reaching down, grabbing bottles of flavored drink, lifting them, and placing them neatly in a line on the shelf of a refrigerated unit. In fact, miles away, there is a human worker controlling the robot's every movement **remotely** via a **virtual reality (VR)** headset. VR allows people to do jobs that require heavy or repeated lifting from the comfort of their own homes or offices.

CLEANING WINDOWS

Many stores now employ robotic cleaners too. Robotic window cleaners work by **suction**, which is powered by a motor. They suck onto the window while they clean using their onboard sensors. These sensors allow the robots to work without any controls.

CLEANING FLOORS

Fully autonomous floor-cleaning robots roam grocery store aisles and scrub the floors. They are fitted with AI systems that enable them to retrace routes that the staff train them to follow.

ROBOTS GO TO SCHOOL

Robots are even taking over schools! Well, not quite, but in the future, you could be seeing a lot more robots in classrooms. Nao (pronounced "now") is an interactive, 23-inch- (58 cm) tall humanoid robot that is already working in many schools as a teaching assistant—with a difference. Nao helps teachers bring lessons to life and teaches students in a new and fun way.

Here and Nao!

Nao is an advanced humanoid robot that has mechanical joints so it can move in a similar way to humans. Nao has cameras and sensors on its feet. It also has **rangefinders** that it uses to see, recognize, and judge distances so it can avoid obstacles. Nao can also pick itself up when it falls. It can reproduce sounds and speech so it can have conversations with people too.

Nao It's Time to Learn

Nao can help teach children to read and write. It can also teach subjects such as math. For example, Nao's storytelling feature means students will be able to program the robot to read stories they have written. Nao has expressive features on its face, such as smiling, which it uses to tell the childrens' stories in an interesting way.

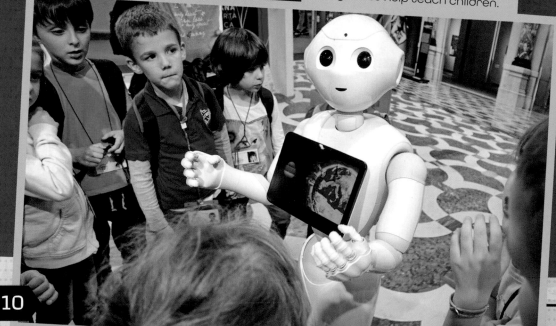

There are a number of different educational robots that are designed to help teach children.

Nao can speak to students in languages including Spanish, French, and Japanese to help them learn other languages.

A Friendly Face

Nao comes with a programming tool designed to allow students to code the robot with **gestures**, movements, sounds, music, and speech. This helps children learn programming and also makes the robot more like a human. People tend to feel more comfortable when they talk to a humanoid robot.

Robot Reassurance

Children who are on the **autism spectrum** often focus their attention more on objects and less on people. They may not speak a lot or they may mimic, or copy, speech. They find comfort in repetitive behaviors. This makes Nao their ideal teacher. Nao can be programmed to have the same, even voice and no confusing facial expressions. It can do the same thing, in the same order, and at the same time every morning. Children respond well to Nao because it is like a toy.

BIG BOT DEBATE

Are Robotic Teachers Good or Bad Educators?

Some people believe that robots can help in classrooms. They argue that children feel less worried about getting something wrong in front of a robot. A child can make any number of mistakes before they get an answer right, and the robot will not react badly. Other people disagree. They say only a human teacher can understand a child's feelings as well as their educational needs. Do you think robotic teachers are good or bad?

Chapter 2

ROBOTS ON THE JOB

Robots can be on the job 24/7, 365 days a year. They just keep working on their own or alongside people in an ever-growing range of industries. Many industries could not survive without their robotic workforce.

UP TO THE JOB

Industrial robots are stronger and fitter than people. They don't risk harming themselves in the workplace by lifting heavy objects or by breathing in harmful paint or glue fumes. They also don't get tired or sick. They just keep going as long as they are checked, oiled, and repaired regularly.

The downsides of industrial robots are that they are expensive to buy and it can cost a lot to train people to use them.

ROBOTS RISING UP!

The fabric uppers on top of Adidas Futurecraft Strung running shoes are not cut into shape and glued onto a sole like regular sneakers. Instead, a robot weaves the Strung fabric from 10 different colors and strengths of thread into a sneaker shape. The robot's arrangement of thousands of threads is based on three-dimensional (3D) scans of the changes in shape of runners' feet as they move. Tougher threads are positioned to give more support and more elastic threads are positioned to allow the shoe to be far more flexible.

The Strung robot can weave a running shoe upper from scratch in a few minutes.

QUALITY CONTROL

Robots do their industrial tasks to a high standard, every time. They have sensors built in to check they are using the right amount of force or materials required. The sensors also check they are making a cut or sticking something on in the right place. This means they make fewer mistakes and there is less waste. They can often do their tasks faster than humans, too.

UNIQUE TALENTS

Some robots have special talents. For example, robots are on the rise in building electronics such as smartphones or tablet computers. These robots can slice and handle fragile, thin **silicon** wafers used to make **circuit boards** inside these electronic devices. Humans could easily break the wafers or spoil them by leaving fingerprints or dust on their surfaces, so using a robot means more parts are made and there are fewer breakages.

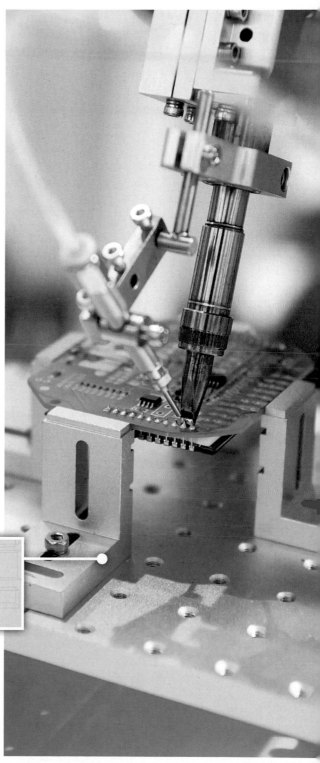

This robot is helping build an electric circuit board at a factory. It handles each fragile part carefully.

Precise **laser** tools used on robotic arms for welding were developed from those used in high-precision eye surgery.

ROBOTS ON AUTO

The one place where you are guaranteed to see robots at work is in an automobile plant, or factory. There are around 1 million of these robots around the world and they work in crews on many important stages of making an automobile.

HOT WORK

Robots handle the incredibly hot, sharp-edged metal pieces that are pressed into vehicle body parts. Robotic arms tipped with lasers blast light beams to heat the metal to very high temperatures at precise locations. They then press the parts together. The robot's sensors are not damaged by the lasers as human eyes could be.

PAINTING VEHICLES

Nearly all automobiles are painted by robots. Robotic arms spray coats of paint onto the bare metal shell of the vehicles. Operators program painting robots using computer 3D models of the automobiles. The program calculates the cheapest, quickest way of coating the model. Then it instructs the arm to paint the actual shell. Each coat is even and the right thickness, so there are no ripples, bubbles, or drips. The first coat prevents the metal from being worn away by water or salt. Then five more coats of paint are usually added, each around the thickness of a human hair. A final coat of paint stops the color from fading.

BRING ON THE FANS!

Fans dry each coat of paint before the next one is added. They also extract any coating spray from the air in the facility to stop it affecting the next coat.

HIGHLY POLISHED

Giving an automobile its gleaming showroom finish can take a human worker hours. A robot can produce a clean and regular shine on every part of the vehicle in far less time. When the robot has finished, there are no areas where it has pressed too hard or not hard enough, which can make the shine on a car uneven.

ROBOTS RISING UP!

Robots are also helping make the high-performance engines of supercars. Solid engine blocks cast from metal have rough surfaces and the car parts would not move properly inside rough holes, so these fast cars would not drive as well. The ARCOS robotic arm effortlessly lifts the heavy block and then moves it onto spinning grinders and polishers. It changes the angle and direction of the block to create mirror-smooth holes ready for moving parts to be added.

A spray attachment on a robotic arm paints every automobile surface evenly.

FANUC
Robot P-50iA

COBOTS ON CALL

Many robotic workers are fenced off from humans. The robots are big, powerful, and fast. These bots are so focused on completing their task that they could accidentally harm humans who get in the way. Collaborative robots, or cobots, are different. They can safely work side-by-side with human workers.

SAFETY FIRST

Cobots are smaller and less powerful than many industrial robots. Even so, they have several safety features to stop them harming their human coworkers. They have cameras and other sensors to detect objects and people around them, so they move in ways to avoid contact. They are also programmed to slow down or shut off immediately in case of an unexpected collision. Cobots have **pressure** sensors to detect whether they are applying too much force in their work, too.

REPETITIVE TASKS

Cobots are equipped to take on the necessary, but less desirable, repetitive tasks on **production lines**. For example, a cobot feels no wrist strain after completing a screwdriving action thousands of times in a day and it can squeeze out just the right amount of glue from a dispensing gun every time.

Maybe one day, cobots will even high-five their human coworkers at the end of the working day!

Robotic suits called exoskeletons give humans robotic powers so they can lift much heavier objects than they would normally be able to.

POWER VEST

Some human workers are gaining the strength of cobots by wearing a robotic exoskeleton, or external skeleton, called VEX. VEX is a harness with joints that mimics the way human arms and shoulders work but without any battery power. Instead, it operates with groups of springs. VEX is designed especially for people doing work with their hands above their heads, such as adding parts to the underside of a car. They need to support loads and be mobile. Someone wearing VEX can do this for longer without having to stop for a break.

ROBOTS RISING UP!

Next-generation cobots may well be Successors. Successor is a system in which cobots learn and reproduce the movements of a human worker. The cobots can then pass on skills to other identical cobots. In this way, a single human operator can operate multiple robots at the same time, even if they are on automobile production lines in different countries.

COBOT ARMS AT WORK

The YuMi cobot is a versatile robotic arm. This means that it can do many different things. It is designed to replace people with machines in production lines in a wide variety of industries. YuMi's arms can be programmed to change function to best suit each task.

Armed and Ready

YuMi is an ultra-light robotic arm that weighs just 21 pounds (9.5 kg). It can operate as a single arm or two arms that work together. The arms are built from metal and can turn in seven ways to copy humanlike movements. All the moving parts are sealed so the fingers of YuMi's coworkers cannot get caught in them and the arm has no sharp corners.

ABB

YuMi stands shoulder to shoulder alongside human workers. It takes on routine tasks allowing people to do more difficult work.

YuMi at Work

YuMi cobots are at work doing many types of small-but-important jobs. For example, YuMi organizes the thousands of **samples** that come into one Swedish blood-testing laboratory each day. YuMi unscrews the tubes that the samples are transported in, scans identification barcodes on the tubes to enter the samples onto a **database**, and then stores the samples ready for doctors to later analyze.

Program and Go

Programming a YuMi is simple. YuMi has a programming system that enables a worker to get the cobot on task in a few minutes. Operators drag-and-drop graphics, or images, of functions they want the arm to do, in the right order. The software helps the user teach the robot movements and positions easily and quickly. Then the arm demonstrates what it has been taught.

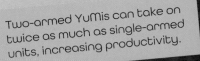

Two-armed YuMis can take on twice as much as single-armed units, increasing productivity.

BIG BOT DEBATE

Are Cobots the Future for Factories?

Some people think that cobots are great. They say they are cheaper, can work on a wide range of tasks, are user friendly, and safer than many other industrial robots. If a task changes over time, a cobot can be reprogrammed in an instant. However, others are not so sure. They argue that cobots will take over so much of a job that there won't be any work left for humans. Do you think cobots bring great advantages or do you believe they pose a threat to the jobs of humans?

ROBOTS WORKING OUTSIDE

Not all industrial robots are trapped inside factories and laboratories. Some have broken free to take on heavy work in the outside world. These awesome bots are changing the way things are done in several different industries.

ON THE BLOCK

Hadrian X is a wall-building bot. It is a truck with a 105-foot (32 m) arm that has a gripper at the end. It can lift and lay blocks to build walls up to the height of a three-story building, with no need for scaffolding. It is doing the heavy, time-consuming work of bricklayers. For thousands of years, walls have been built in the same way: by people stacking bricks or concrete blocks and sticking them together with **mortar**. Now there is a new way.

ROBOTS RISING UP!

Hadrian X constructs buildings. The robot builds walls based on a programmed 3D building design. Hadrian X can be fitted with a saw that can cut blocks into the right length and shape, and it even applies adhesive, or glue, before positioning blocks together.

Demolition robots help construction workers break down old buildings so they can start work on new ones.

GONE TO WASTE

Every year, millions of tons of jumbled waste arrive at recycling centers in the United States. It is dull, dusty, and sometimes dangerous for humans to separate the waste into different types, such as metal, glass, or paper. The ZenRobotics Recycler can sort it more effectively and faster than a human. It has sensors including metal detectors to identify metal, as well as cameras and 3D sensors to analyze the shapes of objects. It can also fire a type of **infrared** light at the waste to sort it based on the different ways that materials absorb the light. Its robotic arms accurately sort the different types of waste 98 percent of the time.

TREE MUNCHER

The Scorpion King from Ponsse is a tree-munching bot! It is an eight-wheeled tractor with an arm that grabs massive trees in a death grip. The head of the arm wraps around the trunk and inbuilt chainsaws slice through the tree. Then the head automatically draws the trunk through grinding teeth that strip bark and branches off the log. The saws then chop the clean trunk into the perfect size to transport.

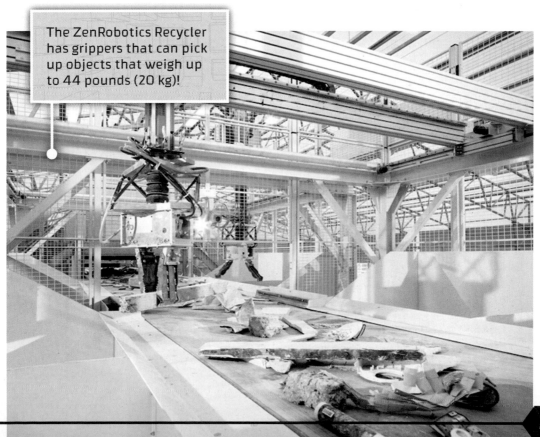

The ZenRobotics Recycler has grippers that can pick up objects that weigh up to 44 pounds (20 kg)!

Chapter 3

ROBOTIC DELIVERY DRIVERS

Industrial robots are not just producing, or making, goods and materials in industries. They are also at work in the next stage: getting the items to the customers. And this work starts in the warehouses and ports of the world.

Robotic warehouse pickers can locate and pick up specific items.

GUIDED TOURS

The products or materials kept in a warehouse are usually ordered in a grid system of horizontal and vertical lines. The system uses the letters x, y, and z, making it easy to command **automatic guided vehicles (AGVs)** to move x rows across and y rows down the warehouse, then move up z shelves to locate the item.

ROBOTS RISING UP!

The Magic Container Terminal is the name given to Yangshan Port in Shanghai, China. Almost no people work there. Instead, hundreds of quayside container cranes for unloading containers off ships, and the AGVs that shift the containers, work automatically. The AGVs follow routes around the port using **GPS** and have sensors to avoid collisions.

The Magic Container Terminal in China is one of the largest automated container ports in the world.

ROUTE MASTER

Many AGVs take routes by following markers or wires set in the warehouse floor. Others have lasers that reflect, or bounce off, mirror tags set around the building. The AGV calculates its position and route using the pattern of the light **coordinates** that it receives.

AGV IDENTIFICATION GUIDE

The AGVs that find and pick the product, move it to a packing area, then load the packaged product on delivery vehicles are not all the same. Mouse AGVs are small, low to the ground, and drive beneath their load. Tugger AGVs are heavier robots that can hitch to carts laden with goods, and tug them to their destination. Turtle AGVs are designed to carry particularly heavy loads, from monster truck tires and rolls of steel to ship containers. Forked AGVs are robotic forklift trucks that can lift or move down goods stacked on flat crates called pallets, to or from locations that are high up.

DELIVERY WITHOUT ANY DRIVERS

Don't be surprised if you see a delivery truck on the road without a driver! The next generation of delivery vehicles is getting by without human drivers on board because they drive themselves.

KEEP ON TRUCKING

Robotic trucks have technology that detects the vehicles around them, what is approaching, and the other vehicles' speed. The trucks use radar and LiDAR to do this.

Radar sends out **radio waves** that bounce off objects. The reflection pattern tells the robot's computer what the object is and gives its position. LiDAR does the same as radar but it uses light. The computer then decides how much the truck steers, speeds up, cruises, or brakes.

STARSHIP IS ON IT!

Next time you order groceries or prepared food online for delivery it may arrive by Starship! Starship robots are advanced, autonomous machines designed to carry food that extra mile to your door.

I deliver to Beavers
www.starship-beavers.com

Food delivery robots bring you a meal and are able to keep it warm until it arrives.

Have you seen the Amazon Scout delivery robots rolling along a sidewalk near you?

ROBOTS RISING UP!

When training robotic trucks to follow routes, operators create events that would change road conditions. They include sudden storms or gusts of wind, unexpected construction zones, and obstacles including broken-down vehicles or pedestrians wandering onto the route. The vehicle is then trained to adapt the way it drives when encountering unexpected conditions.

SLOW AND STEADY

Starship bots are slow and steady, moving at walking pace. They have 12 cameras to see where they are going and can move around objects and people on the sidewalk. They follow GPS-guided routes and have an **insulated** lockable container to keep food fresh. Only the customer can unlock it to get their goods.

DRONE DELIVERY

Delivery vehicles have taken to the skies too! Drones are delivering goods for companies such as Amazon. The drones have several spinning blades to lift off, hover, fly forward, and land. Being off the ground keeps these robots out of the traffic. They have radar and LiDAR sensors to spot obstacles such as chimneys. Amazon Prime Air drones have specially designed blades that reduce noise so people can barely hear them.

Unlike humans, drone delivery robots are never held up by traffic jams or crowded sidewalks, so they deliver more parcels, and quickly.

ROBOTIC SHIPPING

In 2021, a special ship bot set sail in Norway, Europe. The *Yara Birkeland* is the world's first fully electric and self-propelled container ship. Transporting containers on this beast should save 40,000 trips by gas-guzzling trucks a year. Could many autonomous ships like this soon cross the oceans?

Mega Robot

The *Yara Birkeland* is probably one of the biggest robots on Earth. It is about the length of a jumbo jet and slightly wider than the length of a school bus. It is made of tough, heavy steel and can survive the knocks of powerful ocean waves. The ship can carry up to 120 standard containers with a maximum weight of more than 3,440 tons (3,120 mt).

High-Powered Robots

Most ships have engines that burn oil but the *Yara Birkeland* is battery powered. It has two massive rooms filled with high-energy batteries, a little like those that operate the motors on electric automobiles. The battery system has pipes of cooling liquid running through it to stop the batteries overheating. Electric motors produce none of the gases regular ship engines release, which contribute to **climate change**.

This robotic ship will not break speed records! It chugs along at about 7 miles per hour (11 kph).

All by Itself

The *Yara Birkeland* is autonomous. The ship's computer plots the best, safest course, or route, using weather forecasts, radar, and LiDAR. It also has a sonar system. Sonar uses sound waves to find and figure out the location, size, and movement of underwater objects. The *Yara Birkeland* also has an automatic identification system (AIS). It sends up-to-date information on every ship it spots, including its speed and course. This robot always knows what else is on the water.

Are Robotic Ships the Future?

Some people think robotic container ships are good news. We live in a world where labor is in short supply and more goods need to be transported in bulk by ships. Long, slow journeys on established sea routes don't need skilled crew. However, other people disagree. They say it is not safe to let robots take charge of ships weighing many thousands of tons. Experienced crew can keep their ship and other ships they encounter safe. A robotic ship is more likely to be overturned and spill containers or even harmful cargo. Do you think robotic ships are an advantage or do you think they are too dangerous to use?

Chapter 4

ROBOTIC FARMERS

When most of us imagine a farmer, we see a person in outdoor gear, wearing a hat and gloves, hard at work in a field. But on many farms today there are also mechanical members of staff: robotic farmers hard at work in the barns and fields, completing many different tasks efficiently and safely.

HELPING DAIRY FARMERS

On dairy farms, farmers have to fetch herds of cows from the fields twice a day and attach tubes to their teats to get their milk. Even on a small dairy farm, that could mean two people, working 7 days a week, 365 days a year. Robotic milking systems do all this work—alone.

FEEDING TIME

When a cow needs to be milked, she walks to the robotic feeding and milking machine. The robot's sensors identify each individual cow by an electronic tag on the animal. An automatic feeder drops the right amount of food for each particular cow, depending on what she needs.

Robotic milking machines allow cows to come to be milked on their own, when they choose to.

ROBOTS RISING UP!

Not all farm robots work in fields or barns. If you look carefully above some big farms, you might see small drones flying back and forth. These drones are busy gathering images of the farmer's crops. Farmers can use these images to quickly assess crop health so they can make decisions to get the best out of their crops, for example, by adding fertilizers (plant food) to areas of crops that are not growing well.

Drones help farmers by checking how well crops are growing. Others can spray fertilizer over fields to help the plants grow.

MILKING TIME

While the cow is feeding, a robotic arm uses laser technology to locate the cow's udders. Then, it gently attaches the milking pumps to them. The cow stands contented and relaxed, eating the feed provided while she is milked.

UDDER DATA

While the cow is eating and being milked, the robot collects a lot of useful data, or information, about the animal and sends it to the farmer's computer. This information tells the farmer about the cows' health, how often she visits the milking machine, and how much milk she produces each time. If the cow has been milked too recently, an electronic gate allows it out of the stall. Because the robot milks entire herds of cows, robot milking machines leave farmers free to do other work on the farm, such as chores, farm management, and planning.

Driverless tractors have sensors to keep them from bumping into unexpected obstacles.

ROBOTIC TRACTORS

Driverless tractors can move up and down fields autonomously, 24-hours a day, without a farmer anywhere in sight. The fields that the robots work on are first mapped out by drones. Farmers use the information that the drones gather to program the robotic tractors and to plan their work.

WORKING AROUND THE CLOCK

Once the farmer has a plan in place, all they need to do is attach the necessary equipment to the tractor. Robotic tractors can tow plows used for overturning the soil to get it ready for planting. They can have manure spreaders fitted for fertilizing the soil, and seed drills, which sow seeds at equal distances and depths, just like a regular tractor. Then the robot gets to work, traveling backward and forward, for hours at a time.

GOOD REASONS FOR ROBOTS

Robotic tractors don't get tired and can free up time for the farmer to do other work. Another advantage of robotic tractors is that they are much lighter than regular farm machinery. Heavy farm machines squash soil and force out air as they trundle across fields. When soil is heavily squashed, it is more difficult for plants to put down roots. Plants rely on their roots to collect water and nutrients from the ground.

HARVEST TIME

For a long time, most robots were not advanced enough to handle the level of precision needed to select and pick ripe-but-delicate crops such as fruits. Today, robotic pickers are busy gathering fruits that bruise easily, such as strawberries and leafy vegetables like lettuces that are easily torn.

ROBOTS RISING UP!

Lettuce is a difficult crop to harvest. It grows close to the ground, has fragile and easily damaged leaves, and needs to be cut at precise points. Specialized lettuce-harvesting robots use specific calculations to check if a lettuce is healthy. One camera scans the lettuce to check if it is ready to cut. A second camera guides a blade to cut the lettuce without crushing it.

HOW THEY WORK

Harvesting robots are fitted with specific end effectors for the particular crop they are picking, such as gentle graspers and cutters. Computer vision and sensors help the robots identify ripe crops. Then they pluck or cut the fruit from its stem and pack it. Robotic harvesters are a real help in fruit-picking seasons because fruit needs to be picked quickly before it begins to spoil.

The Agrobot's robotic arms can analyze each strawberry before cutting and picking the fruit.

It may seem a calm, quiet day on the farm but out in a field is a killer! It suddenly stops and locks on to its unsuspecting target. Then, its weapon extends and with a brief "pssst" sound, the victim has been sprayed with a deadly mix of chemicals. This sounds like the stuff of nightmares but it is actually one of the latest farm robots in action, killing its enemies—weeds in large fields of crops.

AI in Action

Some weed-killing bots use AI to identify the weeds in a field filled with plants. The robots have AI that helps them learn to tell the difference between crops and weeds, even if the leaf differences are small and the leaves are damaged or positioned at different angles.

Some weed-killing robots also have an **electrode** end effector. Once locked on to a target, it can deliver a powerful electric shock to a weed. The AI ensures a perfect hit and the weed is fried alive from the inside, without damaging any of the valuable food crop plants around it.

LaserWeeder uses AI, lasers, and high-resolution cameras to distinguish between weeds and crops. It is able to kill weeds at any time of the day or night, and in any weather conditions.

The IBEX2 weed-killing robot needs only a few drops of deadly spray to finish off its victims!

Killer Bot on the Loose!

The IBEX2 weed-detecting robot is able to travel autonomously over mud and rough ground in search of its target. It runs on tracks that allow it to work on hilly land, on slopes of up to 45 degrees. It navigates, or finds its way, using GPS, helped by other data from maps and satellite photos. Its software analyzes the images of a plant and, using math, identifies whether or not the plant is a weed. The weeds are targeted using a robotic arm with a spray end effector.

Robots Have the Power

When weed-killing chemicals are sprayed across whole fields, potentially harmful chemicals enter waterways. This can damage plants and animals. Using robots like IBEX2 that can kill individual weeds is better for the environment.

BIG BOT DEBATE

Are Robotic Farmers Good or Bad?

Some people say robotic farm workers save farm owners money, which could make food cheaper. Robots can also reduce the amount of resources used, such as water and chemicals, which is better for the environment. Others disagree. They say that farm robots cost a lot of money to buy and need maintenance to keep them running. They also take jobs away from human workers. Do you think robotic farmers are a good or bad idea?

Chapter 5

ROBOTIC INSPECTORS

Checking dams, power lines, and other **infrastructure** is vital. It prevents explosions, blackouts, and other life-threatening situations. But, having human inspectors is time consuming and dangerous. To get a close look, they have to climb ladders, scaffolding, or cranes, where there is a risk of falling. Robotic inspectors are faster and can go higher or deeper with no risk.

DRONES ON DUTY

Drones can take videos and photos from the air to give a bird's-eye view of the ground. This footage can be used to inspect hard-to-reach objects and locations, such as power lines, railroad tracks, aboveground gas pipelines, and tall construction sites. Some drones inspect power lines and pylons for birds' nests, damage from lightning strikes, rust or other decay, and damaged bolts. The drones use high-quality video cameras and **thermal imaging** cameras that show up spots in the power lines where heat is escaping, which is a sign of damage. Human operators plan the drone's **flight path** in advance and analyze the data it sends back to their computers.

A drone can spot faults early so they can be repaired before they cause problems.

A type of pipe inspection robot is designed to mimic the movement of a caterpillar as it travels inside pipelines. The robot is divided into three sections: one for movement and two for legs that attach to the pipe's inner walls.

Inspection robots have onboard sensors to collect and record information about the condition of pipes.

GAS PIPE INSPECTORS

There are thousands of miles worth of pipes carrying water, waste, oil, and natural gas buried under the ground. Pipe inspection is vital to ensure there are no blockages, cracks, or other issues that could cause problems, pollute the environment, or create disasters. Various types of robot are designed to fit and run inside the sometimes cramped and small spaces inside pipes. These bots inspect the pipes, and include worms and PIGs, which is short for Pipe Inspection Gauge.

WORMS AND PIGS

Worm-type robots move in a similar way to earthworms and can travel through narrow pipes. They stretch so they are longer and thinner, and then become shorter and wider or bend from one side to the other, pulling themselves forward. They move slowly but get to where they need to go. PIG robots are designed to fit larger oil pipelines. Once they have been launched inside a pipe, they are moved along by the force of the liquid traveling through the pipes behind them. As well as inspecting, some PIGs also clean the pipes as they move along.

ROBOTS AT GREAT HEIGHTS

Wind turbines are machines that turn wind energy into electricity and they are often found in areas of high ground or in the ocean. In these places, the spinning blades at the top of the turbine towers get battered by hail, rain, strong winds, and lightning strikes. Checking wind turbine blades so high up is dangerous for human inspectors, so robots are often given the job. These robots use cameras for the inspections, and sensors that can detect faults below the surface.

IS SOMETHING BUGGING YOU?

Six-legged bug drones are taken by larger drones to the turbines. The bug drones grip onto the blade surface and crawl around to inspect different parts of the blades. These robots move by lifting three of their feet at a time, while the other three cling to the surface. Suction cups on the bugs' feet change shape to ensure grip as they crawl. These robots can carry out repairs themselves using a special robotic arm. And they can even check and repair the giant turbine blades when the blades are swooshing through the air.

Blade-inspecting robots remove the danger to humans of inspecting giant turbines.

Robots are replacing humans in the world's mines.

HAZARD WARNING

Autonomous robots are also carrying out inspections in areas of mines that would be too hazardous for humans. Mining robots have sensors to detect objects around them and onboard AI systems that allow them to learn to find their way by building a map of their surroundings. They also have sensors to check for problems. For example, they monitor the air quality and provide warnings about gas leaks that could be dangerous.

CHECKING OLD MINES

Mining companies also use robots to explore old, abandoned mines to find out if they contain valuable **minerals** that weren't useful in the past but may be valuable today. Old mines can be flooded and filled with murky water and there's a risk tunnels will collapse. Sending a robot into those cramped spaces is much safer than sending humans.

ROBOTS RISING UP!

A shopping cart-sized robot named Julius is working alongside humans in mines. This strong, wheeled robot can drive itself, avoid obstacles, and has a robotic arm with a three-fingered hand. It also has spotlights, sensors, scanners, and cameras. It can analyze minerals and collect important information, for example, the air quality in deep parts of a mine.

ROBOT TAKEOVER:
ROBOT SAFETY TEAMS

Flying in an airplane is one of the safest ways to travel because of all the careful inspections that take place. As well as regular safety checks, planes are immediately inspected if there are signs of damage. Damage can be caused by lightning or bird strikes in the air, things on the runway, or accidental collisions with other vehicles.

Flying Inspectors

Some of the robots used to inspect planes are drones, which are used to fly around an aircraft in a hangar or on the runway. These drones follow a pre-set inspection path during which they take images using their onboard camera. The drones' pictures are then transferred to a computer database where they are analyzed. The drones have laser-based sensors to help them avoid obstacles.

Bug Bots

Tiny bug robots are being designed to creep and crawl through the insides of a plane's engine. Once inside, they send live video feeds from small cameras to an operator who inspects the engine. These robots work as a team, scurrying to different parts of the engine and capturing images of what they see.

Robots can check planes for any damage that might be caused by sudden lightning strikes.

Inspection drones can look over an entire aircraft from different angles much more quickly than a human could.

Climb and Cling

To check a plane forced to land after a lightning strike for example, engineers would work on ladders or scaffolding at heights of up to 26 feet (8 m). At that height, a fall could be devastating. Small inspection robots with a suction mechanism can climb up and cling to the outside of an aircraft at any angle, including upside down. These robots have high-quality cameras that can check surfaces for faults such as pits and cracks, which human eyes may not spot. The cameras send video images to engineers on the ground, who figure out if and where repairs are needed.

Are Robot Inspectors Up to the Job?

Some people believe robotic plane inspectors are more reliable than humans because they can work for hours without tiring. Robots can also work autonomously at any time, which makes the job cheaper and quicker. Others say robots are designed to do repeat tasks and are not good at understanding changes that occur around them. They say robots could miss new or unexpected signs that something is wrong, which humans would notice. Do you think robot inspectors are reliable or do you believe they are too risky to use?

Chapter 6

ROBOTS DOING DANGEROUS JOBS

Some jobs are so dangerous that they are near to or beyond the limits of humans. Robots, meanwhile, can survive being exposed to harmful substances such as strong acids in the chemical industry or very explosive substances in industries that supply the military. Working under dangerous conditions, such as very high temperatures, is all in a day's work for robots.

STIRRING HOT POTS

Robotic arms can stir pots of molten, or melted, metal at temperatures greater than the Sun's surface without getting burned. Molten metal contains unwanted solid pieces called slag. In the past, workers would wear protective gear and stir the metal with a pole to remove slag. Stirring the slag creates a shower of hot sparks and clouds of poisonous gases. These workers would face extreme danger in opening a tap hole on the container to let out the molten metal, and to insert a clay plug to seal it again. Today, robotic arms wrapped in heatproof materials do the job instead. They have grippers to hold the stirring pole or the clay-plug injecting tool.

Powerful robots take on high-risk tasks, such as clearing areas of loose rock, to keep people safe.

ROCK STAR

Mining rock is heavy, hazardous work. To reach valuable minerals, miners drill holes, pits, and tunnels, and blast away the rock. Miners face many dangers, including explosions, rock collapse, and breathing in harmful dust. It's no wonder robots are doing more and more of the dirty work in mines. Pit Viper is an enormous drilling rig robot. A drilling rig is a drill mounted on a truck to make deep holes. Pit Viper autonomously drills an exact pattern of same-depth holes in the rock. Explosives in the pits then blast at the same time to break up entire layers of rock —with no humans in sight.

Pit Viper's sensors help it move and operate effortlessly in hazardous mining conditions.

ROBOTS RISING UP!

Fires can rage at industrial sites such as oil refineries or rigs, airports, and chemical plants. These intense fires are far too hot for firefighters to deal with and can produce poisonous clouds. But robots such as TrackReitar are built for the job. This bot has thermal-imaging cameras to detect the sources of greatest heat. TrackReitar aims a water cannon at the source of the fire and sprays 1,270 gallons (4,800 l) per minute to help calm the flames before firefighting crews arrive on the scene.

GOING NUCLEAR

Robots boldly go where few humans dare to enter. Nuclear power plants are potentially very dangerous for human workers. Robots are an important part of the nuclear industry's workforce because they stop human workers being exposed to harmful stages of nuclear power production.

HAZARDOUS PLANTS

Nuclear power plants use heat produced by splitting or fusing atoms to make electricity. This process leaves behind nuclear waste that is highly hazardous. The waste produces radiation, which includes invisible rays that can cause damage as they pass through the human body. It also leaves behind radioactive particles that are dangerous if swallowed or breathed in. To stop radiation effects, nuclear waste is stored for long periods underwater or in concrete containers until it becomes less radioactive.

It's much safer and more efficient for robotic arms to deal with nuclear waste than it is for humans.

ATOMIC WORKERS

Robots are designed with instruments and working parts that are not affected by radiation. Robots can also be used to lift and carry nuclear waste into storage containers. Robotic arms shaped like snakes can wriggle into small openings to make repairs to pipes and other parts of a power plant, using drills, cutters, and grippers.

CLEAN-UP SQUAD

Cleaning a nuclear power station, especially if there has recently been an accident there, is a job no humans would ever want to do. Producing nuclear power leaves work surfaces and equipment coated with radioactive waste that requires a lot of work and chemicals to clean. Instead of humans doing this job, robotic arms have been used to spray surfaces. The latest robots are designed to use powerful lasers to clean nuclear sites more quickly and thoroughly too.

ROBOTS RISING UP!

Lyra is a small robot with a big job. This robot travels through small spaces such as air ducts to check for radiation. It is kitted out with five radiation detectors, two cameras, lights, and an arm that can be used to collect samples of the radioactive contamination from a surface. The robot runs on caterpillar tracks and sits clear of the ground so it can drive over piles of rubble or debris.

Human workers wearing protective gear can safely monitor robots working in a nuclear plant from a distance.

ROBOT TAKEOVER:
IN TOUCHING DISTANCE

Shutting down, or decommissioning, an old nuclear power plant is complicated. The many radioactive parts of the plant need to be collected, sometimes swabbed clean of radioactive dust, cut into pieces, and put into secure storage for tens of years. Only then will they not be a threat to humans. Luckily, a specialist robot with a robotic hand can help with this work. Its name is Shadow Hand.

Virtual Fingers and Thumbs

Shadow Hand uses a special glove to control a robotic hand at the end of a robotic arm. When a person moves the glove, the robotic hand copies the movement. The arm has cameras so operators can see exactly what the hand is doing. A remote operator can make the hand hold tools and move to mop up, chop waste, and detach fixed items. The hand can also pick up different-sized pieces of waste and move them to safety.

Shadow Hand is **dexterous** and can lift objects that weigh up to 11 pounds (5 kg).

Robotic hands may look like something out of a movie but they could be the future of industries where people face real danger.

BIG BOT DEBATE

Fingertip Control

Tactile Telerobot is a version of Shadow Hand that has pressure-sensing fingertips. The remote user can "feel" changes in a series of pads on the glove fingertips. These changes are made by the sensors on the fingertips of the telerobot. The user can feel the shape and consistency of the nuclear waste and sense whether it is stuck to the floor or sharp to touch. A human's protective suit or gloves might get cut by sharp objects, allowing in radiation, but Tactile Telerobot will be unharmed.

Are Robotic Hands Safe or Dangerous?

Some people think robotic hands are the future of dangerous nuclear work. They say robots are the only option to keep people safe. The world is shifting toward different power sources but we still need safely operated nuclear power plants. Others disagree with this. They say any robot can stop working properly and do things it is not programmed to do. What if a robot causes a nuclear accident and radiation is released? Do you think robotic hands help keep people safe or do you think they pose a threat instead?

GLOSSARY

artificial intelligence (AI) the power of a machine to copy intelligent human behavior

autism spectrum a range of conditions that affect the way a person communicates and how they experience the world around them

automatic guided vehicles (AGVs) robots that can move on a specific pre-programmed route

autonomous able to act independently

circuit boards sets of electrical connections made by thin lines of metal fixed onto a surface

climate change the long-term shift in Earth's weather patterns and average temperatures

conveyor belt a continuous moving surface that transports objects from one place to another

coordinates a set of values that show an exact position

database an organized collection of digital information, or data

dexterous having skill and agility with hands

electrode one of the two points through which electricity flows into or out of a battery or other device

flight path the route of a moving object, such as a plane in the air

forklift a vehicle for lifting and transporting heavy objects by means of steel fingers that are put under the load

gestures actions that express a person's feelings or intentions

GPS an acronym for Global Positioning System, a system of satellites that work together to give exact locations on Earth

infrared describes rays of light that feel warm but cannot be seen

infrastructure power supplies, transportation networks, and other important systems

insulated surrounded by a material that stops sound, light, cold, or heat entering or escaping

laser a very narrow beam of highly concentrated light

minerals natural chemical substances that make up rocks

mortar a building material that is used when wet and becomes hard when it dries

pressure a pushing force

production lines lines of machines or workers in a factory along which a product moves

programmed given instructions using computer code

radio waves invisible forms of energy that can carry information and move through the air

rangefinders devices that measure how far away objects are

remotely in a different place, often far away

samples small amounts of something that provide information about it

sensors devices that sense things such as heat or movement

silicon a substance found in sand that is used to make electronic parts

suction a pulling force

thermal imaging able to make images of things we cannot see by sensing the heat they give off

virtual reality (VR) a computer generated world that feels real and can be explored and interacted with by a person

FIND OUT MORE

BOOKS

Andrews, John. *Bots and Bods: How Robots and Humans Work, from the Inside Out*. Andrews McMeel Publishing, 2021.

Idzikowski, Lisa. *Robots in the Factory* (Searchlight Books —Exploring Robotics). Lerner Publishing Group, 2023.

Martin, Claudia. *Robotics in Industry* (Robot Pioneers). Lucent Press, 2018.

WEBSITES

There are more robot facts at:
https://kids.kiddle.co/Robot

Find out more about how robots work at:
https://sciencetrek.org/sciencetrek/topics/robots/facts.cfm

Read more about robots at work at:
www.timeforkids.com/g2/robots-at-work

Publisher's note to educators and parents:
All the websites featured above have been carefully reviewed to ensure that they are suitable for students. However, many websites change often, and we cannot guarantee that a site's future contents will continue to meet our high standards of educational value. Please be advised that students should be closely monitored whenever they access the Internet.

INDEX

ABOUT THE AUTHOR

Louise Spilsbury is an award-winning children's book author who has written hundreds of books about science and technology. In writing and researching this book, she has discovered that robots are rising, revolutionizing our world, and paving the way for an awesome high-tech future!